MW01700124

About the Authors

Charles Poliquin is a world-renowned strength coach and authority on weight training. His training methologies and programs have been credited with countless gold medals, team wins and personal bests. A native of Ottawa, Canada, Coach Poliquin has a master's degree in exercise physiology and the equivalent of a PhD in practical experience as a trainer of champions. His international coaching résumé boasts over 500 Olympians (including nine medal winners at the Lillehammer Olympics), 60 professional hockey players, and world championship professional teams such as the Chicago Bulls and the Denver Broncos.

Art McDermott attended Boston University, completing his BS in education before continuing on for graduate work in exercise physiology. During this period, he became a four-time All-American in track and field. He has published numerous articles in strength-related magazines on a wide variety of topics. At last count, he has participated in 23 national championships in three different sports, and has attended the Indoor World Championships in both track and field (1990) and Scottish Highland Games (1999).

POLIQUIN

Healthy. Lean. Strong.™

Art McDermott and Charles Poliquin

Contents

POLIQUIN

Healthy. Lean. Strong.™

An Introduction to Applied Strongman Training for Sport

As strongman training becomes increasingly popular as a modality for athletic preparation, it is vital to understand why it works.

This chapter might have been more appropriately titled "True Functional Training for Sport," but the term *functional training* has been so widely misinterpreted that an incorrect association would have been unavoidable. As such, clarification is in order.

Many coaches have mistakenly considered the expression *core training* to be synonymous with *functional training*. They believe that if you are training the musculature of the torso (such as the rectus abdominus, transverse abdominus, and internal and external obliques), you are creating a better-functioning athlete and therefore are doing functional training. This is not the case.

Core training strictly strengthens the abdominals. While strengthening these muscles is important, it is only one aspect of the larger picture. The fact is that core training should not dominate the program design, as often occurs in many facilities, both private and institutional. Direct abdominal training need only be addressed periodically throughout the yearly cycle. With correct program design, coupled with proper technique, abdominal musculature is adequately recruited by execution of the major strength movements – in addition through sport participation during the remaining yearly cycle.

Functional training should be defined as the execution of movements directly related to the patterns required for a given sport, with the obvious intent of improving athletic performance. The ineffectiveness of some popular approaches in the functional preparation of athletes is due to several causes, including the following:

1) Most approaches to functional training are inadequate because the resistance used is insufficient. Studies have shown that resistance below 60 percent, unless accompanied by accommodating methods such as heavy-duty bands and chains, does not sufficiently stimulate muscle tissue to promote strength gains.

2) The patterns commonly employed in functional-training programs do not resemble "on field" conditions. Exercises performed on unstable apparatus such as physio balls,

wobble boards and thick padding are best left to rehab work because in competitive activities there are very few surfaces that move in such a manner.

3) The use of physio balls, balance boards, light "thera" bands and other such apparatus can generate some abdominal stimulation but does not produce a sport-specific training effect. These tools do have a useful place in the direct training of the abdominals and, again, as part of a rehab program, but they have limited use beyond this in any athletic preparation program. They are incapable of developing any usable strength.

As a consequence of poorly designed functional-training programs using the above concepts, we are seeing a wave of athletes who have sufficient abdominal strength but who are remarkably weak. "Abs and Rehab" would be an appropriate slogan to reflect a more appropriate outlook concerning the proper use for the ubiquitous physio ball and its derivatives. Claims for any use beyond that serve only to sustain an entire industry built upon the sale of ineffective gadgets and gizmos.

Unfortunately, the belief that such items are necessary tools for strength and speed development has been successfully instilled in the minds of coaches and parents everywhere. But the truth is that a stronger athlete, given the presence of well-developed sport technique, is a superior athlete. This is particularly true for contact sports.

It is our belief that modified strongman training is a far more effective approach for attaining usable strength. As such, this coursework will address the use of the Farmer's Walk, Super Yoke, Log Press, Tire Flip and Sled Pulling, as well as their various combinations, as an athletic preparation modality. Their proper use is based upon the following concepts:

1) True functional training can only be achieved while using significant and adjustable resistance while executing sport-specific movements.

2) The outcome of the proper application of modified strongman training is usable strength, which will prove particularly valuable in contact sports such as hockey, football, rugby, martial arts, wrestling, basketball and others.

3) The use of these methods can be seen in two general forms: a) sport-specific, as mentioned, and b) as part of a general preparation process for most sports.

4) All of the exercises described here should be treated just like any major weightroom movement such as the squat or power clean with regard to progression, technique development, safety concerns, periodization and recovery.

Although limited research exists involving these techniques, the steady increase of their use in major collegiate programs and professional settings is testament to their usefulness. Coaches at this level cannot afford to waste valuable preparation time with inferior methods. The superior techniques of modified strongman training can be seen in the preparation of teams at the University of Iowa; University of Nevada, Las Vegas; and Arizona State University, as well as professional players in the NFL, NHL, MLB and a variety of Olympic sports.

Prior to implementing any of the routines or techniques described herein, it is important to understand that that these movements are neither more nor less dangerous than any other demanding strength movement. As such they require sufficient knowledge of technique as well as extensive awareness of safety issues. The bottom line: Train hard, but train smart!

POLIQUIN

Healthy. Lean. Strong.™

Chapter 1 • Sled Work

Objectives

- **Understand the equipment**
- **Identify specific sports the event will benefit**
- **Identify the muscle groups worked**
- **Learn specific exercise options**

Background

The inspiration for the use of sled work for sports can be loosely traced to the Scandinavian forestry industry. Once a tree was felled, loggers would drag it from the wooded areas not accessible by vehicles. Louie Simmons, powerlifting coach extraordinaire, brought sled dragging to the forefront by drawing this information from the Finnish powerlifters when querying them regarding their deadlifting prowess. They claimed that their background in dragging trees from logging employment provided them with a solid base of posterior chain development, which is key to excelling in the deadlift.

This two-post, reversible sled has the simple and versatile design needed for any surface and any athletic population.

If you were dumped on a deserted island and were allowed only one piece of exercise equipment, it should be the sled because virtually every muscle can be trained using this apparatus. And the more resistance the athlete has to overcome in his or her sport, the more useful the sled, which is why it is a strength tool of choice for rugby and football players. Sled work is also useful in other team sports such as basketball, ice hockey, soccer and volleyball.

Special Advantages of Sled Work

Injury Rehabilitation. Sled work provides one of the best forms of strengthening the vastus medialis muscle in a progressive but non-impact manner. In contrast to squatting, sled work can be done early in the rehab process. Forward and Backwards Sled Walking are also more inherently natural movements than squatting, and therefore they can be done shortly after orthopedic surgery once medical clearance for any resisted movements is given.

Muscular Balance Diagnosis. Several of the exercises described in this course provide important feedback with regard to the structural balance status of an athlete. For example, if an athlete is executing a Petersen Drag and consistently drags or pulls the sled off a straight line towards one side or the other, this fault may indicate a piriformis that either is too tight or is too strong relative to the opposite side. Similar diagnoses can be performed for muscle groups such as the hamstrings by using the One-Arm Drag. This diagnostic tool underscores the concept of true functional training, which is executing real-world movements against adequate resistance.

Functional Hamstring Work. Even though leg curls and various forms of deadlifts, pulls and good mornings will develop an excellent base of hamstring strength, sled work will permit the athlete to transform that base into usable strength on the sports surface.

Lateral Speed Improvement. Sled work is the fastest way to develop lateral speed. The strength coach must realize that lateral speed is almost always expressed in a situation where inertia has to be overcome; hence the need for load. No amount of speed ladder training can match the results of sled work.

The sled is the only practical tool that can overload hip adduction and abduction patterns in a positive functional way. The more commonly used bands placed around the ankles or legs are inadequate because there is no quantifiable way to measure or increase resistance in controlled increments.

Skating Power. Korean short-track speed skaters use the dragging of tires to improve skating power. Using a sled permits athletes to have a more gradual and quantifiable increase in resistance. We use it extensively with NHL players and Olympic speed skating medalists, with very appreciable results.

Energy System Training. Many of our pro athletes use sled work as their primary form of energy system work for sport-specific preparation. The following four energy systems can be trained using the sled: 1) anaerobic alactic power, 2) anaerobic alactic capacity, 3) anaerobic lactic power and 4) anaerobic lactic capacity.

A great sled from Elite Fitness

General Technical Concepts

The preferred surface will minimize friction so the load can be more closely controlled by plate loading versus estimates of surface friction. For example, an asphalt or concrete surface works ideally. It has been our experience that sleds with a "dual runner" design do not adapt well to various surfaces. The steel, flat-bottomed design of the sled shown above will easily meet the needs of personal trainers, strength coaches and professional strength athletes.

Regarding footwear, for Backwards Sled Dragging, hiking boots are the footwear of choice because of the loads involved. For lateral work, best results are achieved with plain sneakers or tennis shoes, as they force the athlete to stabilize the ankles.

The sled provides innumerable options to increase the variety of exercises that can be performed, such as the following:

- **Forward Facing**
- **Hands Together, V-grip**
- **Waist Belt Point of Contact**
- **Backwards Facing**
- **Hands Separate, Rope Grip**
- **Ankle Point of Contact**

Because of the specific nature of each exercise and the versatility of the sled, there are no universal technical points that apply to all sled work. Even the grip used to hold the straps is not universal, although as a guiding rule the grip should be specific to the sport being trained. If a given sport has a strong grip component, such as hockey or wrestling, then emphasis should be placed on requiring a more active grip on the strap as opposed to a passive loop attachment around the wrist.

Sled Exercises

The Petersen Drag. Note that the range of motion is very short. The most common mistake is to take too big a step

Petersen Drag

This is the sled variation of the Petersen Step-up used in rehabilitating the vastus medialis, a teardrop-shaped muscle that crosses the knee joint. It is also a great exercise for athletes who need to rebalance their knee tracking because of overwork of the vastus lateralis, including alpine skiers, speed/figure skaters and hockey players. Some prefer to call this exercise the Moonwalk Drag.

Description

Stand facing the sled holding one handle per hand. Nylon straps with sewn-in loop handles will work best here.

Place the ball of the right foot just behind the left heel so there is a slight bend in the right leg at the knee. The heel should be lifted to as steep an angle as possible.

The foot must be turned out at a slight angle, roughly 15 degrees.

Apply downward and forward pressure with the ball of the right foot to break inertia of the sled.

Emphasis should be placed upon driving the heel to the ground as rapidly as possible, coupled with an equally rapid extension of the rear knee and foot.

The left foot comes off the ground passively.

Once the right foot is completely flat on the ground, place the ball of the left foot just behind the right heel.

Apply downward and forward pressure with the ball of the left foot to break inertia of the sled.

Continue alternating between the right foot and the left foot until the prescribed distance is covered.

This exercise can be done with the handles held in the hands or with a waist attachment as seen above. There will be superior quad recruitment with the waist attachment, however.

The trunk of the body must remain upright at all times. If the trunk leans back, the resistance is too high and muscles other than the vastus medialis are being recruited.

Always wait for the sled to be immobile before initiating the action of the subsequent step.

There is no need to execute this movement in a rapid fashion. Properly reset after every repetition.

This movement is generally limited to an accumulation (strength building) phase.

This exercise should always be performed with the passive grip around the wrist to promote focus on the vastus medialis without loss of neural drive to the forearms.

Standard Backwards Sled Drag position

Backwards Drag

In our experience, there are very few exercises capable of generating high lactic acid levels and muscular fatigue as rapidly as Backwards Sled Dragging. As a consequence, this exercise should always be placed at the end of the workout, if possible. Refer to the end of this chapter for appropriate sets, reps and distances.

Description

Stand facing the sled with one handle in each hand. Nylon straps, a waist attachment or V-grip handles may be used here.

Lean the torso back slightly.

Drive back forcefully with one foot and then the other in an alternating pattern.

Avoid turnout of the toes of either foot, which usually indicates excessively tight lateral hamstrings.

With lighter loads, it is possible to stay on the toes (quadriceps/gastro focus), but heavier loads will require a toe-to-heel pattern for the feet (posterior chain focus).

It is important to keep the upper body "quiet" rather than use an exaggerated swing of the shoulders to gain momentum.

Standard Backwards Sled Drag position continued

The Backwards Sled Drag with waist attachment is preferred if superior quadriceps isolation is desired

Move the feet as rapidly as possible over the prescribed distance.

If a waist attachment is used, the upper body mass can no longer counter the sled weight and hence the entire load is focused upon the quadriceps; this significantly increases the difficulty of the exercise.

Nose-to-Sky position, with heel drive emphasis

Nose-to-Sky Backwards Drag

Description

This is performed in the same manner as the standard Backwards Drag but with the head tilted back, looking straight upwards.

Attention should be paid to driving through a firmly planted heel.

Emphasis is almost entirely on the vastus lateralis and the posterior chain.

Single-Arm Backwards Drag

Description

Use the same body positioning as in the regular Backwards Drags, but only one hand should be in contact with a handle.

This hand may have both straps in it or be gripping only one side of a V-grip handle.

The free hand should be on the hip; it should not be used to gain momentum through unnecessary movement or as a counterbalance (this would defeat the purpose of a unilateral movement).

Move the feet as rapidly as possible over the prescribed distance; this technique forces asymmetrical compensation of the torso muscles, which mimics many of the

Incorrect free hand position for the One-Arm Backwards Sled Drag. The free hand should remain on the hip.

unilateral situations seen under competition conditions such as throwing a ball or virtually any striking or hitting sport.

Athletes will note superior torso/hip stabilizer recruitment on the side of the body opposite the one holding the handle, most notably the contralateral oblique, quadratus lumborum and gluteus medius.

Bent-Over Hamstring Drag

Both of the hamstring movements described below can be combined very effectively in a *super set* or alternating fashion with leg curls to assure complete hamstring recruitment.

This great exercise is a Louis Simmons original – without a doubt, this is one of the best hamstring builders out there, hence making it an excellent posterior chain strengthening exercise.

Description

Stand facing away from the sled, holding one handle strap and with the arms running along either side of the body.

Bend forward at the waist until the trunk is parallel to the ground, keeping a slight arch in the lower back.

Walk forward for the prescribed distance.

Correct position for the Bent-Over Hamstring Drag

Every attempt should be made to prevent the knee from bending in this exercise, although a slight knee bend is usually unavoidable during the push-off and recovery point of the stride.

The leg is brought forward by using the hip flexors in what is described as a "Frankenstein walk."

Effort must be made not to swing the legs out to the side when pulling either leg forward into the next stride.

The athlete should be cued to attempt to walk a straight line in a rapid heel-to-toe fashion.

The coach must make certain that no excessive shoulder movement occurs during the exercise.

Correct position for the One-Arm Hamstring Drag

SINGLE-ARM HAMSTRING DRAG

This exercise is quite possibly the best unilateral isolation movement for the hamstrings.

It is performed with the same torso position as the standard Hamstring Drag, but only one arm holds the sled strap attachment.

The free hand must remain fixed on the hip or with the thumb looped in the waistband or even in the same-side pocket. Unlike the Single-Arm Backwards Drag, this movement focuses the load on the ipsilateral, or same-side, leg.

The most commonly seen error with this movement is external rotation of the opposing leg in an attempt to recruit the glutes for added assistance. The coach must make certain the opposite side foot and leg remain facing forward.

It is easy to exceed the sufficient load on this movement. If a straight and forward alignment of shoulders, hips and legs cannot be maintained, the load must be reduced.

Start/finish position for Upright Sideways Ankle Drag (top)
Midpoint of Upright Sideways Ankle Drag (bottom)

Upright Sideways Ankle Drag

All sideways dragging movements are strongly recommended for hockey goalies, tennis players, basketball players, football linemen and linebackers where rapid lateral movements are vital.

Description

By using either an ankle cuff with a clip or by forming a nylon strap loop, fix the straps to the ankle.

Make certain a protective layer of cloth or sock is between the nylon and the skin.

Bend the knees slightly while facing perpendicular to the sled.

Push the lead leg – the leg facing the direction of movement – out as far as is comfortable and then pull the trailing leg back under the body to the original starting position.

It is important not to lift the lead leg up into the air and "press" the leg forward, as this technique uses an entirely different set of muscles. This is the most commonly seen execution error. An effective auditory coaching cue is to instruct the athlete to "hover" the feet only inches from the surface of the ground.

The toe of the lead leg must be turned inward in a pigeon-toed manner. This will activate the abductors directly.

Staying low in the shuffle or in an athletic "ready" position, move the feet as rapidly as possible over the prescribed distance.

Most athletes and coaches will have seen this exercise at some point in the past, usually done with a rubber band. The sled is preferred here due to its adjustable nature.

Start/Finish position for Bent-Over Sideways Ankle Drag (left)
Midpoint of Bent-Over Sideways Ankle Drag (right)

Variation 1 - Bent-Over Sideways Ankle Drag

This is a variation of the previous exercise, the only difference being that the athlete is bent forward at the waist until the trunk of the body is nearly parallel to the ground. This position increases the isolation of the adductors and hence the difficulty of the exercise.

Start/finish position of the Sideways Sled Drag with Hand Hold (top)
Midpoint position for Sideways Sled Drag with Hand Hold (bottom)

Variation 2 - Sideways Sled Drag with Hand Hold

Description

Using the same foot pattern as above, the athlete holds the straps in the hands as opposed to having them fixed at the ankles.

Resistance must now be translated through the torso.

While it is less intensive on the hip abductors, it does work the important torso muscles responsible for lateral changes of direction.

The "lead" arm should have the strap in hand and remain bent at the elbow at a 90 degree angle, in a position flat against the torso.

The trailing arm should be fully extended towards the direction of the sled.

Carioca

This old football favorite goes by different names: Crazy Legs or Grapevines, to name a few.

Description

Use only a very light load here, as the tempo is quite fast, ideally with only one leg in contact with the ground at any given moment.

If the speed of the movement drops to a plodding motion, cease the exercise immediately and reduce the load before continuing.

Move as rapidly as possible over the prescribed distance.

This movement should only be used during an accumulation phase.

Start/finish position for the Carioca (left)
Midpoint position for the Carioca, with one leg crossed in front of the other (right)

Pull-Through, Arched Back

This exercise is another Louie Simmons movement. It is an outstanding exercise for developing explosive starts by focusing on the hips and lower back from a dead stop.

Description

Stand facing away from the sled, holding one handle per hand.

Straddle the straps.

Bend forward at the waist until the trunk is at least parallel to the ground, keeping a slight arch in the lower back.

When the nylon strap is pulled tight, the elbows should be at a position even with the inside of the knees.

From this position, forcefully stand upright by firing the hips through to full extension. Do not use the biceps and/or deltoids as primary movers here.

Start position for the Flat-Back Pull-Through (left) and Rounded Back Pull-Through (Middle)
Finish position is consistent for all Pull-Through exercises (right)

The hands should remain in very close contact to the front of the body at the end of the concentric movement. The most common error seen here is to use the arms to pull the load forward. The coach should cue the athlete to use the arms only as an attachment to the sled.

Pull-Through, Rounded Back

This is a variation of the above meant to develop explosive starts. Because of the rounded back position, the erector spinae tend to take a greater percentage of the load.

Description

Stand facing away from the sled, holding one handle per hand.

Straddle the strap and bend forward at the waist while rounding the back.

Bring the feet as far forward as possible so that the athlete is bent over at the waist as far as flexibility allows.

The further the hands can reach back between the legs, the better the range of motion.

The elbows should be adjacent to the knees at the very least.

From this position, come upright as rapidly as possible, moving the hands forward.

It is important not to use the biceps and deltoids as primary movers here.

The hands should remain as close as possible to the body at all times.

Note: Make sure someone is standing between the athlete and the sled to decelerate it as it comes near the ankles, particularly during warm-ups. Once the training weight has been selected correctly, this should not be a problem, as the sled should stop short of the ankles at the end of the Pull-Through.

Shotokan Backwards Walk

This variation requires a bit more coordination than most of the other exercises described here, and aims at working the hip extensor chain. It can also be done with a waist attachment.

Description

Face the sled, with the ankles set in each looped stirrup.

Extend the right leg back, while the right arm is extended in front.

At this point the straps should be taut.

Begin the exercise by moving the left leg back. As you do this, simultaneously extend the left arm forward in a punching-type movement while pulling the right wrist back towards the waist.

This movement would be difficult to replicate with any other form of resistance.

The follow-through punch and step for the Shotokan Backwards Walk

Four phases of the Claw Walk

Claw Walk

This outstanding glute/hamstring exercise can be thought of as an exaggerated form of Lunge Walking.

Description

a. Face away from the sled, a handle in each hand and the hands down at the side.

b. While bending the right knee, lift this leg up so that the thigh is above parallel to the ground.

c. Then extend the knee and reach forward as far as possible with the leg.

d. Once the leg contacts the ground in a long lunge position, use only the hamstrings/ glutes of the forward leg to pull the body forward and return to an upright position with the feet together.

Repeat with the left leg. Be certain to come to a complete stop between repetitions.

The start, mid-point and recovery positions of the Lunge Walk.

Lunge Walk

Description

Same as previous but with a simple reach forward with the forward leg, without the exaggerated knee raise and reach.

Start position for the Face Pull (left)
Finish position with alternating foot position for the Face Pull (right)

Step Back and Face Pull

This movement is used mainly by grappling-sports participants.

Description

Stand facing the sled, holding a handle in each hand.

Start with the feet offset.

Step backwards using the right leg while pulling explosively on the straps in a rowing motion towards the face.

Repeat the pattern by alternating with the left leg.

Three-point stance Blast Start position

Blast Starts

This exercise should only be done by "non-skill" football position athletes and by throwers, powerlifters, Olympic lifters, and martial artists. It is for athletes in sports requiring refined sprinting skills, such as track and field sprinters. Running backs, corner backs and receivers should stay away from this exercise, as it will disrupt their running mechanics.

Sled running should be a definite no-no for anybody who needs to run at high velocities. Some conditioning coaches promote what is referred to as the "10 percent rule," saying that 10 percent of bodyweight should be the maximal load when running with the sled. We strongly argue that sprinting with *any* resistance only serves to compromise running mechanics and to introduce improper motor patterns.

Description

Attach a weighted sled to the athlete at the waist.

The athlete then assumes a three- or four-point stance.

On the signal, the athlete sprints forward as explosively as possible for a distance of 5-10 yards.

This movement can be used quite effectively in "cluster" form, where maximal blasts are done with rest periods of only 15 seconds and sets not exceeding 5 repetitions.

3- to 5-yard sprint position for Blast Start

As an example of how to use this exercise, with football linemen a long series of downs would be duplicated in the following manner:

Execute 12 consecutive 10-yard Blast Starts with 30 seconds of rest between repetitions.

Repeat this sequence multiple times with 5 minutes of rest between sets.

Blast Starts, Upright Start

This is the same exercise as above but with a standing start. This start will increase the difficulty of the exercise because the line of force is farther away from the horizontal direction of pull. This is the preferred option for throwers and martial artists, who must display rapid acceleration in a more upright position than linemen.

Start position of the Sled Row (left) – Finish position of the Sled Row (right)

Sled Row

This exercise is an excellent variation of the standard Low Cable Row. It forces the athlete to stabilize against the ground forces acting in the opposing direction of the pull.

Description

The athlete grabs the nylon straps (straps are preferred because they allow a more natural line of pull versus the close-grip handle).

The knees are bent, and the back is kept flat.

The athlete then forcefully pulls back on the straps, focusing on squeezing the shoulder blades together and pulling the arms to either side of the rib cage.

At the same time, the hips must extend in order to create the necessary lean to maintain balance against the inertia of the sled.

Strength Ratings

These figures completely depend on ground surface and type of sled; therefore we cannot recommend normative data on strength ratings. This is the only event for which we cannot recommend specific standards due to equipment and environmental variations. As a rough guideline, however, here are some ranges for training on a hard surface such as asphalt with a "standard" flat sled such as the Elite Fitness (Louie Simmons) model. These ranges apply only to Backwards Drags, Hamstring Drags and Pull-Throughs. The weights prescribed refer to the total weight of the sled and its contents. All other exercises and low-level recovery work will use lighter loads.

One fact that should be noted right away is that these numbers imply that the athlete should be able to use roughly the same load for Hamstring Drags and Pull-Throughs. The athlete should then be within 15-20 percent of the appropriate weight used for the Backwards Drag. The inability to do so may be an indicator of a muscular imbalance.

Approximate weights for Backwards Sled Drags. Surface friction and sled variety will affect these figures significantly.

Smaller females	**150-200 lbs**
High school males and female strength athletes	**200-350 lbs**
Collegiate males	**350-500 lbs**
Pro athletes and male strength athletes	**500 lbs and above**

Routines and Progressions

Sample A

This routine was prescribed by Charles Poliquin to Dallas Drake of the St. Louis Blues in a phase where Drake needed extra leg work in the evening to regain hypertrophy following knee surgery.

1. Warm-up
2. Set 1: Petersen Sled dragging 6 x 50 yards
   Pressure is put on the ball of the foot

   Rest 5 minutes between sets
3. Rest 10 minutes with PNF stretching
4. Set 2: Backwards Pulling, 4x100 yards
   Lean back 45 degrees; apply pressure with heel of foot

   Rest 4 minutes between sets
5. Warm-down + static stretching

SAMPLE B

This routine was given to Jim McKenzie, Stanley Cup winner, enforcer (sorry, *role player*) of the New Jersey Devils.

1. Warm-up

2. Set 1: Side Dragging, 6 sets x 60 yards x 2 sides
pull 60 yards leading with left
pull 60 yards leading with right

    Rest 5 minutes between sets

3. Rest 10 minutes with PNF stretching

4. Set 2: Step Backs and Face Pulls, 4 x 80 yards

    Rest 4 minutes between sets

5. Warm-down + static stretching

SAMPLE C

This routine combines the Farmer's Walk (as discussed in Chapter 3) and sled work. It was used by Jerry Ostrowski, offensive lineman of the Buffalo Bills

1. Warm-up

2. Set 1: Farmer's Walk, even carrying, 6 x 100 yards
Minimum weight: 150 lbs per hand

    Rest 5 minutes between sets

3. Rest 10 minutes with PNF stretching

4. Set 2: Nose-to-Sky Pulling, 5 x 100 yards
Lean back 45 degrees, apply pressure with heel of foot

    Rest 4 minutes between sets

5. Warm-down + static stretching

POLIQUIN

Healthy. Lean. Strong.™

Chapter 2 • The Farmer's Walk

Objectives

- **Understand the equipment**
- **Identify the muscle groups worked**
- **Identify specific sports the event will benefit**
- **Learn specific exercise options**
- **Learn the world records and current record holders of the event**

Background

The Farmer's Walk (FW) has the longest history of all the strongman events covered in this course. Its origins go back hundreds of years to agricultural Scotland, at a time when it was common to have numerous tests of strength at local festivals and fairs. The name alone indicates these roots, although it has been said that most farmers would likely have had more sense than to perform this event with any regularity unless absolutely necessary.

The current world record in the Farmer's Walk is held by Hugo Girard of Canada. He carried two 175-kilo implements over a 25-meter course in just over 21 seconds! This was made even more difficult because he was competing on a grass surface, which requires significantly more effort. Although inconsistencies in course length, apparatus design and the amount of weight used make direct comparisons difficult, Girard's results are presently the agreed-upon criteria for record purposes.

Equipment

As a rule, Farmer's Walk implements consist of two handles attached to two larger, cylinder-shaped main sections. The main section can be either a fixed-weight object, such as an oxygen tank, or, more practically, plate-loaded posts. These posts are carried parallel to the ground and must be long enough so as not to interfere with the stride of the user.

Surfaces and Footwear

The Farmer's Walk can be performed on multiple surfaces depending upon the goal of the training. As mentioned, a grass surface will increase the difficulty and instability of the stride. This may be desired for rehab situations or with athletes who have demonstrated weakened ankle

Farmer's Walk implements

joints in need of training. For example, alpine skiers and figure skaters often report very weak ankles from wearing equipment that limits ankle mobility for their long competitive seasons. The same applies to ice hockey players. We recommend that ice hockey players spend several weeks each year doing "remedial" loads in the FW in bare feet on a surface such as grass or artificial turf. This will force the firing of lower-leg stabilizers, such as the flexor hallicus longus, which may become considerably weakened throughout the competitive season. Under "standard conditions" with healthy athletes, hiking or work boots are preferred, as higher loads can be used without danger of rolling an ankle.

A change in training surface is recommended for all athletes using this tool regularly. That being said, it is necessary to consider the type of apparatus used when training on hard surfaces, as unexpected drops are inevitable and damage to the training surface will occur unless precautions are taken. Bumper plates as loading implements are the preferred option in this case.

Special Advantages of the Farmer's Walk

Re-establishment of Leg Structural Balance. The Farmer's Walk can be helpful to athletes in virtually all sports, particularly those involving the lower body and torso. This, of course, covers most sports. It is especially useful for contact sports. Because it is a unilateral exercise, the Farmer's Walk is an outstanding tool for addressing muscular imbalances, particularly any weak links in the posterior chain. Because many sports require one side of the athlete's body to be dominant over the other, it is crucial that precautions be taken to prevent uneven development, which could lead to injury. Progress in this exercise will be limited to the weaker side of the body or to the weaker leg, forcing the weaker side to catch up to its more highly developed counterpart on the opposite side.

Vastus Medialis Strengthening. The Farmer's Walk is particularly useful in strengthening the vastus medialis oblique (VMO), a teardrop-shaped muscle that crosses the knee joint and thus is extremely important in maintaining knee stability and preventing ACL injuries. The VMO is probably one of the most undertrained muscles among American athletes, and in our practice we rarely see American athletes with sufficient strength in this muscle group.

Improved Running Speeds. The VMO plays a critical role during the stance phase in running, which is the time spent on the ground with each stride. The stronger the VMO, the shorter the stance phase, as the switch between the eccentric and concentric phases of contraction is shortened. This translates into faster running speeds.

Ankle Strengthening. The Farmer's Walk is one of the very few movements available that can help effectively strengthen the ankles. It is our contention that the Farmer's Walk is superior to methods commonly used for this purpose, such as wobble boards, which do not duplicate the normal motor unit firing pattern found during movement with or against load on a field, court or other competitive surface. Most of our athletes report high levels of delayed-onset soreness in the musculature of the lower leg the very first time they use the Farmer's Walk.

Spine Rebalancing. The load used may also be manipulated to recruit fibers from one side of the body over the other; for example, loading more weight on the left apparatus than on the right. This is useful in cases where the oblique or erector spinae muscles demonstrate an imbalance, such as often occurs with shot-putters. A right-handed shot-putter will often have an imbalance throughout the torso in the obliques, erectors and quadratus lumborum due to the unilateral firing patterns and load of this event. If left unchecked, this type of imbalance could become a limiting factor in performing squats or other major lifts, possibly resulting in an injury.

One notoriously weak muscle group, the rhomboids, is very effectively targeted during standard Farmer's Walk exercises. Strengthening this muscle group can be a quick step towards improved results in exercises requiring a fixed back position, such as deadlifts and squats.

Technical Points

Unless the athlete is performing the Timed Holds that are described in this section, the execution of the Farmer's Walk should employ rapid footwork. The increased speed of execution will increase the tendency towards instability of the movement, hence requiring more-rapid adjustments on the part of the athlete to compensate. It is this whole-body stabilization effort that generates the training effect.

Basic Execution

The liftoff of the Farmer's Walk is crucial, and should be executed in a deadlift style with a straight back, using a slight arch to avoid injury.

The body should be in an upright position with a slight lean forward

The feet should be directly underneath the shoulders. However, an offset foot placement can be used for special purposes described below. Here, one foot is set forward of the other in the "set" position.

Hand placement is usually dictated by the type of handles on the apparatus but should be centered. This will result in a tilting of the weight forward towards the strongest part of the grip.

If the rear of the hand is in need of rehab or strengthening, the grip position can be shifted toward the forward part of the grip handle. This will tilt the entire apparatus backwards, hence training the third and fourth fingers.

Several types of grips can be used during the Farmer's Walk: a hook grip as used in weightlifting; a thumbless grip where the thumb is not wrapped around the handle but instead is kept adjacent to the index finger; and a standard wraparound grip, where the thumb is wrapped around and rests on top of the index finger and possibly the middle finger.

Stride length should be a normal, fast walking gate. Overstriding will result in an unnecessary turning of the hips, which has little training benefit and could result in injury, even with light loads.

Note: It is very important to maintain contracted abdominals during liftoff and throughout the length of the carry. A momentary relaxation of the abdominals would result in a type of injury similar to what happens when an athlete relaxes the trunk muscles during a squat, because the supportive musculature of the spine would then be required to bear the entire load.

Proper start position for the Farmer's Walk

Strength Ratings

Weights recorded are generally referred to as the starting weight used in one-hand events only, and intensity is based upon 100 percent of the maximal load moved for 100 feet, without dropping the implements. Coaches and athletes should strive for loads equaling their 5-repetition maximum (RM) in the full back squat for the total weight of handles as a work weight goal for Straight Forward Walks. Superior athletes will use greater than this percentage. It is not uncommon to see 115-120 percent of bodyweight per hand for testing purposes.

The starting weight should be roughly 100 pounds per hand for healthy, inexperienced male athletes. For female athletes 75 pounds should be sufficient. Use up to only bodyweight total for unbalanced work for the purpose of increasing unilateral firing patterns, such as 125 pounds on the right side and 75 pounds on the left side left side for a 200-pound athlete. Unbalanced work with loads exceeding bodyweight should be performed only with very experienced athletes and with much caution, with the upper limit at 50 percent max intensity for unstable work.

Farmer's Walk Exercises

Start position for the Farmer's Walk Side Bend

Farmer's Walk Side Bend

This exercise is often used as a warm-up, and it is a safer variation of a one-arm deadlift for oblique and lower back work. It is quite similar to a simple dumbbell side bend, but a greater load is tolerated with the FW apparatus.

The exercise is performed with the athlete holding only one FW handle at a time.

Middle position for Farmer's Walk Side Bend

Description

The athlete should only grasp the implement on the opposite side of the body to be trained, holding the implement suitcase-style to the outside of the leg.

Unlock the knee adjacent to the implement for increased range of motion.

The weight is then lowered towards the floor from a standing position as far as the athlete's range of motion will allow, moving only through a frontal plane.

The athlete then returns to a standing position.

Mid-stride position for Forward Starts and Stops. Note the movement of the implements, which will be similar for the Reverse Starts and Stops

Forward Starts and Stops

Using two FW handles, the athlete initiates a walk and then stops suddenly and is forced to decelerate the weight of the apparatus. Before complete control is regained, the athlete rapidly accelerates again, once more forcing stabilizing corrections.

Mid-stride position for Forward Starts and Stops. Note the movement of the implements, which will be similar for the Reverse Starts and Stops

Reverse Start and Stop

Same as above, but performed while moving backwards.

Start position for the Farmer's Walk version of the Petersen step-up

Petersen Walk

Description. This exercise is the strongman version of the Petersen Step-up

Stand with equally weighted Farmer's Walk implements in each hand.

Place the ball of the right foot just behind the left heel so that there is a slight bend in the right leg at the knee. The heel should be lifted to as steep an angle as possible.

The foot must be turned out at a slight angle, roughly 15 degrees.

Apply downward and forward pressure with the ball of the right foot to break inertia.

End position for the Farmer's Walk version of the Petersen step-up.

Emphasis should be placed upon driving the heel to the ground as rapidly as possible coupled with an equally rapid extension of the rear knee and foot.

The left foot comes off the ground passively.

Once the right foot is completely flat on the ground, place the ball of the left foot just behind the right heel.

Apply downward and forward pressure with the ball of the left foot to break inertia.

Continue alternating between the right foot and the left foot until the prescribed distance is covered.

Timed Holds

This exercise is also referred to as the Finnish Method, as it is routinely used by strongman competitors in Finland, where lengthy outdoor walks are not always an option due to inclement weather conditions. These are performed with the athlete simply standing in place, picking up the handles and holding them as long as possible. This exercise is mentally challenging and is easily quantifiable, and thus creates an instant competitive situation for increased training intensity within a training group.

Unbalanced Walks

These exercises are used primarily to correct muscular imbalances, or in rehabilitation of trunk musculature tears at lighter loads, or to prepare an athlete for future training that requires increased torso demands for athletes such as throwers, grapplers and weightlifters.

This can be performed with either one or two implements.

In the single-implement version, only one hand holds an implement as the other hand is held out to the side as a minimal counterweight.

In the two-hand version, the athlete loads one implement with slightly more weight than the other, and the athlete executes the walk with the exact same technique as the standard walk.

The focus is on the firing of the torso musculature on the opposite side of the body from either the single implement or opposite the more heavily weighted implement in the two-implement version.

Straight Forward Run/Walk for Distance/Time

These highly quantifiable tests are performed with a straight forward carry for a set distance for time or for a maximal distance with a set weight. This is the safest version of the Farmer's Walk and is the one that should be used for testing purposes. This exercise can also be performed with a more natural offset-foot start, which allows for a quick transition to a normal gait after liftoff.

Farmer's Walk on Grass

This exercise is an excellent off-season exercise for sports such as hockey and figure skating in which the foot is held in a fixed position inside a boot or skate. It can be considered "pre-hab" in nature.

The same technique is applied as seen in the Straight Forward Walk, and attention is focused upon a complete extension at the ankle with a rapid turnover of strides.

Offset-foot start position for the Farmer's Walk

Hill Climb

Hill Runs or Climbs with the FW implements will shift the emphasis from the quadriceps to the glutes very effectively. Ascending hills with this form of implement is much safer than some other options such as barbells, which can compromise athlete safety during execution. These are generally performed for a set distance (the height of the hill or stairs) for the fastest time.

Accumulation Work or Strength Phase

Definition: 30 to 65 percent of maximum intensity. The minimal distance for FW work is usually 100 feet, unless unusual circumstances dictate otherwise. For higher-volume work, distances of up to 250 feet are used. The time under tension should be 30-40 seconds and above.

Intensification Work or Power Phase

Use 66 to 100 percent of maximal intensity. The longest distance used should be up to 100-125 feet. The time under tension should be less than 30 seconds.

Timed Holds should use the one-minute mark as a maximal mark. Loads resulting in times above this mark should be increased for improved results. Loads here are generally in the 100-125 percent of maximal-intensity range.

Sample Routine - Accumulation Phase

Petersen Walk

5 x 120 feet @ 30 percent of maximal intensity

Rest 2-3 minutes

Standard Walk

5 x 250 feet @ 50 percent of maximal intensity

Rest 90-120 seconds

Sample Routine - Power Phase

Standard Walk

3-4 x 100 feet @ 90-100 percent of maximal intensity

Rest 4-5 minutes between sets

Offset-Foot Start

3-4 x 100 feet @ 80-85 percent of maximal intensity

Rest 3-4 minutes between sets

Timed Hold

2 x max time @ 120 percent of maximal intensity

Rest 2 minutes between sets

Upper Back/General Torso Pre/Rehab

(only after medical clearance for weight training has been given!)

Unbalanced Walk

2 x 200 feet with 65% of bodyweight on one side and 35% of bodyweight on the other

Rest 2-3 minutes

2 x 200 feet with weights reversed

Rest 10 minutes, including PNF stretching for torso

2 x 200 feet Forward Starts and Stops

Rest 2-3 minutes

2 x 200 feet Backward Starts and Stops

POLIQUIN

Healthy. Lean. Strong.™

Chapter 3 • Super Yolk

Objectives

Learn background information about the event

Learn the technical applications of the equipment

Identify specific sports the event will benefit

Learn specific exercise options

Learn the "best performances" in event competition

Background

The term *yoke* is quite ancient. To this day, a yoke is commonly attached to cattle in order to use them to haul a particular load. It has been used (and still is in some areas of the world) as a feasible way for people to haul heavy loads, such as water and crops, over long distances. This standard usage was later greatly exaggerated in strongman contests to test overall body strength, and it remains one of the foremost tests of torso strength known.

The currently recognized world record in the Super Yoke is held by Dan Ford from the United States. He carried a yoke weighing 1,245 pounds a distance of 5 meters at Venice Beach, California, in April 2004.

One unexpected function demonstrated by the Super Yoke is its ability to help identify athletic talent. In general, individuals thicker through the torso will have initial advantages here, but superior athletes will quickly excel. The Super Yoke is arguably the most challenging of the tools described here because it requires a keen sense of multiplanar, unilateral proprioception (or body awareness). That is, the athlete must constantly correct his or her position under the load while moving forward as quickly as possible. Only athletes with a combination of superior torso strength, reaction time and kinesthetic awareness will accomplish this with any kind of success. Therefore it is very effective in evaluating athletic talent.

It is all too common to see athletes who are very impressive in the weightroom but who cannot demonstrate a high level of skill on the football field. It is our experience that athletes who perform well with the Super Yoke also excel on the football field.

The Super Yoke

Equipment

At this time, there is no set standard for yoke design. As long as the structure is safe during the pickup, carry and drop phases, there is almost no limit to the variations in yoke design used in training situations as well as in competition.

Footwear and Surface

As previously mentioned, the Super Yoke is an outstanding tool for strength development in the torso. Therefore, only well-constructed hiking-type shoes or boots should be worn.

Do not use this tool to train ankle stabilization as described earlier in the Farmer's Walk chapter. There is too much danger of ankle injury.

It is, however, recommended that a variety of surface areas be used for training to provide varied trunk stabilization feedback. Grass, AstroTurf, field turf, asphalt and cement are the preferred choices.

Special Advantages of the Super Yoke

Transfer to the Squat and Deadlift. We have many athletes report poundage increases in the squat by just training the lower body exclusively with the Super Yoke and Farmer's Walk, while abstaining from squat work. One common statement heard from the athletes is that if the Super Yoke is going well, everything is going well.

Sports Application. The Super Yoke is an effective tool for virtually any sport; however, the transfer is especially notable with contact sports such as rugby and American football.

Technical Points

When designing a program including Super Yoke work, the coach must be vigilant with the athlete's readiness, general strength levels and training volume. Our experience has shown that setting specific minimums for use of this tool is not possible due to the great variability among individuals and their innate athletic abilities.

It is possible to develop knee joint irritation and possibly shin splints if this tool is overused or executed with improper technique on a hard surface. If a particular athlete has a history of shin or knee problems, consult a licensed health professional who will correct your biomechanics.

Progressions in this exercise should follow the same slow, steady pattern as would be seen in a squat or Olympic lift so that the load used does not exceed the ability of the athlete. Progressions in this exercise should proceed from light, short walks (50 feet or less), to light, long "runs" (100 feet). *Light* here is defined as roughly bodyweight for a male or female athlete. As a general rule, "runs" of more than 100 feet are only done for accumulation phase work in straight runs described below.

In general there are two mindsets possible for a given Super Yoke session. The first approach is used when the requirement is for the athlete to use as heavy a load as possible for a set distance. During this run, the goal is to prevent the apparatus from moving off-line by firing the torso stabilizers to prevent unnecessary movement. For this goal, hand placement should be straight out to the side with the hands in contact with the uprights. The athlete then uses the shoulder girdle and torso to hold the entire apparatus steady during the forward movement.

The second approach is to intentionally create an unstable apparatus and to force the athlete to correct his or her body position against the subsequent ground forces generated. This is achieved by moving the hand placement away from the uprights and onto the crossbar, allowing a pendulum-type movement of the support base of the yoke. This is why we have hand placement on the side uprights, with the higher hand placement, creating instability. Unlike in the Farmer's Walk, little advantage has been seen using uneven loading patterns diagonally on the loading pins or left-to-right uneven loading.

Basic Execution

The stride used should always be a normal walking gait – do not overstride. The foot placement should be a tight, straight line. An uneven gait will result if the feet fall in too wide a pattern off an imaginary straight line in front of the athlete. The glutes should remain contracted to keep the hips in line, directly underneath the shoulders.

As with most lower body exercises, the abdominals should remain tight throughout the entire run. A momentary relaxation of the abdominals could result in low back injury. This is no different than a heavy squat with regard to torso stability. In fact, it is this forced contraction against ground forces that produces the training effect of this exercise.

The height of the crossbar should be at pectoral height for liftoff. As a rule, the longer the upright or pendulum portion, the more unstable the load becomes, as the distance is greater from the load to the supporting crossbar. If a more stable load is desired, the crossbar should be lower. Be aware, however, that a lower crossbar results in a substantially more difficult liftoff. The eyes should be looking straight ahead, never at the ground.

The coach or observer can prevent injury to athletes by watching for the following key indicators: posture and pace. The load used should be modified if the pace is below that of a quick, steady gait. Because we are attempting to train torso strength in reaction to a normal competitive situation, to deviate too much from a somewhat accelerated walking pace can negate this training effect. A heavy footfall is one good indicator of excessive load. The stride should be heel-to-toes with a quick and almost silent turnover of steps.

Improper posture should be an easy flaw to spot. If an athlete cannot maintain an upright posture with the hips in line with the shoulders, injury may result. A forward lean is not a desired technique here. Decrease the load used immediately if the back begins to lean forward of perpendicular. Be aware that supportive gear can mask the presence of both of these faults and should therefore never be used. Knee wraps may be acceptable for heavier sets – again, no different from heavy squats. In general, belts are only used by competitive strongmen. Their use negates the training effect on the torso.

Correct walking position with abdominals strongly contracted and pushed outward.

Start position for Blast Start with Offset Feet; one foot is placed behind the other

BLAST START WITH OFFSET FEET

In this exercise, the athlete starts with the feet offset, with one foot clearly behind the other, so that a running stride is achieved more quickly. This type of exercise is often used as part of a complex, to be discussed in a later chapter. This movement is only done for 3-5 yards at a time.

From this starting position of the Heavy Support, the athlete simply stands erect

Heavy Support or Bottom-Position Squat

This exercise involves simply standing up with a given load. This is usually performed at a position just above parallel, and heavy weights can be used. The Super Yoke has excellent transfer for developing explosive strength for powerful starts or vertical takeoffs like the ones necessary for blocking in volleyball. The advantage here is that the apparatus can be dropped without regard for damage to a lifting bar or power rack. The yokes are designed to be dropped to the ground. In addition, the instability demonstrated by the yoke at liftoff will work the stabilizers in a way not possible with regular bars.

Mid-stride position for Forward Start and Stop. Note the movement of the implements, which will be similar for the Reverse Starts and Stop

Forward Start and Stop

This exercise is directly applicable to contact sports in which an athletes must resist opposing forces attempting to move him or her against their will, such as when an ice hockey defenseman gets exposed to when protecting the goal. To perform the Forward Stop and Start the athlete intentionally begins to walk forward and then suddenly stops the yoke. The swinging action of

Mid-stride position for Forward Start and Stop. Note the movement of the implements, which will be similar for the Reverse Start and Stop

the yoke will force the athlete to correct their balance in order not to be thrown out of position by the weight, an effect that develops excellent core strength. To make the exercise even more sport specific, a coach can shout "Stop" at random intervals, thereby requiring unannounced corrective measures. This exercise can also be performed moving backwards, which is called the Reverse Start and Stop, and works an entirely different set of corrective movements.

After standing erect, the athlete performs this exercise by stepping sideways as shown

Sideways and Diagonal Start and Stop

This is a tremendous core exercise, especially for the oblique muscles that are often neglected in many strength and conditioning programs. It also strongly works the adductors and abductors of the hips. After standing erect with the yoke, the athlete takes short steps, side to side, trying to keep the crossbar parallel to the ground.

The mid-point position for this variation of the Side-to-Side Walk.

Side-to-Side Walks with Distinct Pendulum Motion

Another great exercise for the core muscles and the adductors and abductors of the hips. For this exercise the athlete stands erect, then walks sideways, using a distinct pendulum motion to increase the involvement of the obliques.

The Zercher Carry

Zercher Carry

Any exercise done in a Zercher position refers to the bar being held in the bend of the elbow instead of a standard shoulder position. The arms are bent at 90 degrees. The hands are then generally locked together for stability and arms are locked in close to the abdominals. This holding position is very challenging and will shift the load being carried from the spine to the upper back and arms. The position is quite commonly used in strongman shows as part of the Conan's Wheel event. The Super Yoke can now be adapted to strengthen the upper back and the biceps. In this manner, athletes who may be unable to carry the apparatus on the shoulders due to flexibility or injury issues can reap the benefits of the exercises described above by using this unique support position

Strength Ratings

A target goal of the trainee should be 1RM in the full Back Squat at the 100-feet intensity level detailed below. Better athletes will use significantly more than this. It is not uncommon to see 2.5 or 3 times bodyweight used in testing scenarios.

Intensity. Maximal intensity for the Super Yoke can be defined as the maximal load moved for 100 feet without dropping the apparatus.

Starting Point. An average, healthy athlete should be able to support their own bodyweight for a total load in this exercise. This includes the weight of the apparatus. For any variation of instability work, up to a bodyweight total, load should be the target. The upper limit for unstable work can be defined as 50 percent of maximal intensity.

Accumulation Work. Thirty to 65 percent of maximal intensity. The minimum distance is 100 feet. Distances of up to 250 feet are employed here in order to generate a time under tension of 30 to 40 seconds. The number of sets is determined by the requirements of that sport.

Intensification Work. Eighty to 125 percent of maximal intensity. Minimum distance is 15 feet, up to a maximum of 100 feet. Time under tension is kept to less than 20 seconds. Again, sets are determined by sport-specific parameters.

Sample Workouts

Football Lineman

Forward bursts @ 80-85 percent maximum intensity x 15 feet x 6 sets with 30 seconds of rest between runs

Rest 180 seconds

Repeat once

This routine could be used as an integral part of leg day. It should be used at the beginning of the workout to assure that the vital stabilizer muscles are not fatigued for this activity. Injury could result doing Yoke work with a fatigued torso.

Hockey

Perform in succession:

Backward Walks: 50 feet @ 45-50 percent max intensity

Sideways Starts and Stops: 50 feet

Forward Burst: 100 feet

Drop the yoke on the ground to reposition for next phase

Total time: 1:00 to 1:15 minutes

Repeat 10-12 times for energy system training

Be certain to move in each sideways direction an equal number of times

POLIQUIN

Healthy. Lean. Strong.™

Chapter 4 • Log Pressing

Objectives:

- **•Understand the background of the event**
- **•Identify specific sports the event will benefit**
- **•Understand specific sport applications**
- **•Learn specific exercise options**

Background

This strongman event started in the 1970s as a standard test of shoulder strength. Prior to becoming popular as a competitive event, Log Pressing was often used by military forces to develop overall strength. Its use by weightlifters for general physical preparation purposes goes back to at least the beginning of the last century. For obvious reasons logs are readily available training implements in rural areas.

Prior to the 1950s the bench press was virtually unheard of and overhead pressing was the method routinely used to improve upper body strength levels. In fact, weightlifting competitions used to have an overhead press as a primary event until 1972, when it was eliminated due to the difficulty in judging the movement and because having three events significantly extended the length of competitions. Anecdotally, there were far fewer rotator cuff injuries prior to the use of the bench press as the staple for upper body strength testing. This is because the neutral anatomical grip of the Log Press is actually much more biomechanically suitable for the shoulder girdle than the internally rotated position associated with the bench press, and therefore it is less stressful on the wrists.

A typical design of the training log

Equipment

The Log Press is optimally performed on an apparatus with handles recessed into holes carved in the wood or, more realistically, cut into a hollow steel or aluminum tube. These handles generally run perpendicular to the length of the log. The distance between the handles can vary considerably, but 22 inches apart is a generally accepted standard. The overall length of the log can also vary, but generally it does not exceed eight feet and can be as short as four to five feet. The longer the log, the more difficult it is to control, creating an additional training effect. The logs are generally from 6 to 14 inches in diameter. All logs should be plate loadable for practicality.

We strongly discourage the use of a lifting belt while training with this exercise, as the belt would negate the core strengthening effects of the Log Press. In addition, unlike in other exercises discussed in this book, in the Log Press there is no benefit to performing this movement on an uneven or unstable surface. The existing recruitment of the stabilizers is sufficient.

Special Advantages of the Log Press

Total Body Exercise. A large amount of muscle is used during the Log Press, especially when a full clean and press movement is performed. In overhead Log Presses the upper back must stabilize the torso in concert with the abdominals on the opposite side of the body.

Functional Training. Novices using the Log Press will immediately notice the need for superior rhomboid strength when training with the apparatus. The log is a more transferable movement pattern for football players and many other athletes when performing clean and press movements, and there is significantly more biceps involvement in the clean and press movement due to the neutral hand placement. All of these results can be attributed to the awkwardness of the apparatus itself. "Odd object" lifting has found a place in many sports training programs in recent years. This family of movements produces muscle recruitment not seen with more balanced barbell exercises, and that certainly is not possible with machine-based exercise movements.

Rehabilitation. After an athlete receives medical clearance for rehabilitation purposes, the Log Press should be reintroduced into training before any back-supported pressing movements such as the bench press and incline bench press. This approach will enable the trunk stabilizers to be more fully developed before other higher-load upper body lifts are reintroduced.

Core Training. The Log Press has an advantage over Olympic bar pressing due to a greater recruitment of the torso stabilizers; incidentally, the need for stability in the torso muscles increases in proportion to the diameter of the log. Additionally, because the center of mass of the log is farther away from the lifter's own center of gravity than with a regular barbell, there is an increased lower back recruitment. It is not uncommon for an athlete unfamiliar with Log Pressing to experience considerable soreness in their abdominal muscles after an initial Log Pressing training session.

Bench Press Transfer. Overhead Pressing transfers to increased bench press strength, but the reverse is not true. Trainees often report personal records in the bench press after dedication to increasing Log Pressing weights, concurrent with abstinence from bench pressing.

EXERCISES

INERTIA PRESS IN POWER RACK

Also known as a Bottom Position Press, this exercise is performed in the power rack with the log fixed so that the handles of the log are at forehead height when the log is resting in the rack. The lifter may be in a seated or in a standing position. From here, the log is pressed to a fully locked position overhead. This is a superior way to develop the triceps and shoulder musculature.

Consider that any form of Log Press can be performed inertia-style in the power rack. In other words, Flat, Decline or Incline Presses can be done with the log within the power rack. Practical experience has shown that band work, as promoted extensively by Louie Simmons and the lifters at Westside Barbell, works extremely well with Inertia Pressing with the log.

We suggest that the log be placed motionless on the pins for a count of two seconds to eliminate any muscle stretch-reflex in the lift. This trains the lifter in the ability to overcome inertia, which has great application for the shot put athlete, for example, but is equally true for football lineman and powerlifters. Because of the relative instability caused by the handle grip, the Inertia Press is an effective way to strengthen the wrists in both the ulna and radial flexion planes.

Start position of an Incline Inertia Press

Finish position of the Incline Inertia Press

JERK

This lift is performed in the same manner as a barbell jerk from the rack. From a standing position (the bar can be cleaned to this position or taken from a rack), the athlete drives the bar up overhead using an initial knee bend. Once the hips, knees and ankles are at full extension, the lifter drops under the bar using either a split or power drop. If a Split Jerk is used, be certain to alternate between the left foot and the right foot as the forward foot in an equal number of sets; this lift is completed when the feet are brought back to a side-by-side position.

It should be noted that due to the thickness of the log, a significant movement of the head is required to protect the chin when lifting the log to the overhead position. Many a chin has been inadvertently clipped during execution.

The ready position for the Military Press, Push Jerk, Power Jerk and Split Jerk exercises

The catch position of the Split Jerk prior to recovery

Elbows-locked finish position for all Overhead Presses

Push Press

With this exercise the log is pressed overhead after an initial push from the legs. After this initial knee extension, no re-bend is allowed in the knee in the Push Press (in comparison to the Jerk) so as to place more emphasis on the shoulder muscles.

Military Press

Here the log is pressed overhead without any assistance whatsoever from the legs. The lift may be performed while standing or seated, but standing is preferred in order to retain the upper back involvement.

Clean and Press

While the pressing portion of this lift has been described above, the clean movement is significantly different from that of a normal barbell lift. The log does not revolve and has a much larger diameter than the barbell. Hence, the movement is more of a roll up of the abdominals and chest of the lifter to a position on the front deltoids, which teaches the trainee how to use the hips to throw the mass of the log upwards towards the chest.

Start position with the bar on the floor

Power Clean position with log resting on the lap

Start position for a Band Lockout with the Log

Finish position for a Band Lockout with the Log

Band Lockout with the Log

This exercise is a direct modification of the bench press band lockouts used at Westside Barbell Club. They do a great job of training acceleration at the top of the lift, as the athlete is aware that the bands will make lockout extremely difficult if the load is not moved rapidly. The following are the steps to perform it properly:

Set up a log in the power rack at roughly forehead height.

Adjust the bands so there is some tension at the bottom position.

While standing, rapidly drive the log to an overhead lockout position.

Hold the lockout for three seconds, and then return the log to the support pins under control.

After a 2-second pause, press the log up again.

Start position for Reverse Band Press

Finish position for Reverse Band Press

Reverse Band Press in Rack

There may be situations when overloading the lockout position of a Standing Press needs extra attention. For this exercise, place the log in the power rack resting in bands that have been suspended from the top of the rack. A similar approach has been used by lifters at West Side Barbell with the Deadlift and Bench Press for quite some time.

As the weight increases, the log will descend lower and lower as the bands are stretched. Due to the assistance from the bands, the lifter need only support a portion of the entire weight of the log when it is in the shoulder position. This makes the initial movement much easier, and the lifter will be able to lock out in the vicinity of 115-125 percent of his or her regular pressing max. Because the drive is much more powerful and faster, the lifter can handle more weight. Locking out this supramaximal weight can also have a significant positive impact on confidence levels.

Start position for Bent-Over Row. Log is just clear of the floor

Start position of the Inertia Bent-Over Row with the log resting on the platform

Finish position for both the Inertia Bent-Over Row and regular Bent-Over Row

Bent-Over Row

This lift is performed exactly like the barbell version but with the neutral grip. The elbow flexors are at their strongest involvement; therefore, more load can be handled and more resistance is provided for back development. The increased log diameter, however, provides a significant challenge. This lift will fatigue the lower back area much more than the barbell version. This fact needs to be considered during program design.

Inertia Bent-Over Row

This is the explosive version of the lift above. This version has the advantages of relieving the lower back of its supportive duties while training explosive power in the same muscle group. With the log starting on the floor, the lifter dynamically pulls the log to the chest and then lowers it again to the floor.

Clean and Press for Time

This is a great conditioner for athletes in mixed martial arts and grappling sports, and in fact it can be used as a predictor of sport-specific fitness for those sports.

The athlete is given a set time period within which he or she must execute as many repetitions in the full Clean and Press as possible. It is important here that the log be fully locked out and that the log touch the ground between every repetition (see sample program below).

Log Jammer

This excellent exercise has great transfer to any sport where rapid explosion is necessary. Track and field athletes have been doing variations of this exercise for ages employing barbells, logs and medicine balls. Relatively light weights are used. This exercise requires a padded landing area or a sandpit and is performed as follows:

First, clean the log to the lap position.

Next, roll the log up to the chest position, then drive the arms, hips and legs to full extension at approximately a 45 degree angle, throwing the log into the landing area.

The coach needs to make certain that the athlete uses high speed to execute the major portions of the lift in order to recruit the fast twitch fibers.

Strength Ratings

When the apparatus is held on the chest with knees locked, the male athlete should be able to use 66 percent of his best Bench Press performance for the same number of reps. Female athletes would use 45 percent of their best Bench Press performance for the same number of reps.

Routines and Progressions

Offensive Linemen

Inertia Incline Press in the Power Rack

6 sets of 2-3 reps on a 22X0 tempo; rest 4 minutes between sets

This will develop explosive strength, as inertia has to be overcome on every rep

Mixed Martial Artists

Clean and Press for Time

6 sets of 15 seconds of work; rest 120 seconds between sets

This will develop alactic capacity because of the incomplete rest intervals

Chapter 5 • Tire Flipping

Objectives

- **Understand the equipment**
- **Identify specific sports the event will benefit**
- **Identify the muscle groups worked**

Background

Perhaps the easiest piece of equipment to acquire, and the one most likely to provide the highest return, is the tire. The sets and reps in Tire Flipping are extremely easy to manipulate for anything from pure power work to extended lactic-acid training.

The posterior chain is remarkably well targeted during Tire Flipping. The exercise has therefore been correctly prescribed for sports requiring sprint speed and explosive movements with the hips in addition to its obvious benefits for energy system work. Perhaps the only other functional training tool that can be compared to Tire Flipping is the "lumberjack" tool popularized by Canadian Olympic lifting coach Pierre Roy (see Appendix B).

Tires come in a variety of sizes

Equipment

Used tires are considered hazardous waste, and therefore truck tire dealers are eager to get rid of these. You should never have to pay for a used tire. The only downside of the equipment is that there is no consistency among different used tires of the same model, as matching sets are virtually nonexistent. And while methods have been described regarding adding weight to existing tires by the use of sandbags or by bolting plates inside the tires, neither method is recommended or very practical.

One of the most important factors in tire selection is the profile, or width, of the tire; this is the height of the tire as it rests flat on the ground, on its side. As a general rule, tires having a width of less than 20 inches are too low to achieve a safe position for either male or female athletes because the athlete's chin should be resting on or just above the top surface at the start of the drive phase. The chest and upper arms of the athlete must be resting solidly against the side of the tire as well. If the chest extends too far above the height of the tire, the arms are forced to bear too much of the actual tire weight and injury can easily result. Ideally, the chest should be the point through which the majority of the force passes to the tire.

It must be kept in mind that tires vary considerably in diameter, thickness, content (e.g., steel-belted radial), wear, tread design and texture. Here are some rough guidelines for selecting the correct tire weight:

325 to 400 pounds for women and smaller male high school athletes

400 to 600 pounds for larger high school and collegiate athletes or for professional women strength athletes

600+ pounds for collegiate linemen and professional athletes

Tires below these ranges have very little training value. Athletes who find that tires below 300 pounds in weight are difficult to work with are not physically prepared for tire training. In contrast, tires in excess of 700 pounds should be considered excessive for collegiate athletes, given the potential for injury versus possible training benefit.

The classic incorrect start position for Tire Flipping with high hips and excessively wide foot stance.

Technique

Multiple articles have been circulated recently depicting horrendous techniques being employed while flipping the tire. The most common error is that of an athlete addressing the tire with the hands inside the legs, the back in a sumo deadlift-type position and the feet very close to the base of the tire. This position results in a line of pull that is quite close to the vertical. Such a line of force has resulted in many torn biceps tendons. This is the single most common injury associated with Tire Flipping.

The correct approach is to lean the chest into the tire and move the feet back to roughly 2-3 feet away from the base of the tire, depending upon the overall height of the athlete. Grasp the tire with the hands on the outside of the legs, as this position will encourage an automatic forward lean into the tire.

When the athlete is in the correct position, the athlete's chin should rest on the top surface of the tire. Keeping the hips low, the athlete will drive the hips, knees and ankles to full extension. If this action sounds remarkably like an Olympic lift, then you have a correct understanding of the movement. Once the triple extension is complete, the athlete should then be able to drop into the catch, or transition, position. This largely requires the feet to move into a split recovery-type position and the hands to move from an underhand start position to an overhand driving position. The athlete then drives the base of the hands forcefully into the tire and pushes it over end to the ground once again.

The correct start position for safe Tire Flipping

The triple extension position for the Tire Flip, after the initial hip drive

Again, do not attempt to use the biceps to lift the tire from a low position, as a biceps tear can easily result. It is generally not considered wise to biceps curl 500+ pounds. As stated above, biceps injuries are the single most reported injury with this tool.

The transition position with dynamic knee drive

The transition position of the Tire Flip without knee strike during the knee drive

The catch position

The arm drive finish position

Special Advantages of the Tire Flip

Sports Training. There are very few sports for which the Tire Flipping exercise would not be applicable. For example, in soccer, with its lower-body-only involvement, athletes would likely derive less-than-optimal benefit. Due to the low pulling position involved, basketball players are another group for whom tire training would be impractical. Athletes in most other sports would possibly derive some benefit from tire work.

Energy System Training. The tire is arguably the top endurance training and/or functional training exercise for American football, rugby and mixed martial arts athletes. It should be considered one of the top endurance exercises in general. There are still some outdated football coaches using a 1.5-mile run for linemen as a test of fitness and mental toughness – aerobic testing for football makes as much sense as giving a Japanese exam to measure German language knowledge! It has zero value and has a high risk of injurying the larger athletes.

If one wishes to argue that aerobic testing is a test of mental toughness for linemen, we would counter that the athlete who guts out the last three flips of a 10-flip series with an 800-pound-plus tire has superior toughness over the athlete who plods through the last 200 yards of a 1.5-mile run. In short, the tire training exercise tests both preparedness and mental toughness far better than other age-old techniques, especially aerobics.

Routines and Progressions

Suicides

For this routine three athletes take turns flipping the tire without rest. Each athlete performs 3-5 rapid flips, and the next athlete then steps in and continues the rotation.

Repeat 12-15 times for conditioning

Interval Training

30 seconds (roughly 4-6 flips)

Rest 90 seconds

Repeat 3-4 sets

Power Training

3-5 flips for shortest time

Rest 3-5 minutes

Repeat 5-6 sets

Chapter 6 • Endurance Complexes

Objectives

Learn how strongman events can be combined to increase local muscular endurance

Learn how to employ the laws of specificity with strongman training while increasing local muscular endurance

Course Summary

One unique aspect of functional strongman training is its versatility. Because the modality itself is based on true functional movements using various objects and implements in a more realistic competition environment, the training becomes highly transferable to athletics. This is crucial when dealing with sport-specific endurance.

Studies have shown that in order for energy system training to benefit a given sport, the method used to develop this energy system must be as closely related to the sporting movement as possible. It has been well documented in scientific literature that energy system adaptations are not only central but also peripheral. For example, training on a bike to improve endurance for a kayaking event is somewhat limited in effectiveness by its lack of specificity.

Having athletes perform aerobic training on a treadmill despite the fact that it does not resemble their sport movements can largely be a waste of time. This is especially true for sports (such as wrestling) that involve a wide cross-section of different muscle groups and where endurance is needed in multiple planes. It makes more sense to have athletes in such sports use more-functional energy system work, particularly in a collegiate environment, where training hours often can be limited by class schedules or even NCAA regulations.

With these concepts in mind, the strongman events discussed here can be combined to form the basis of an endurance training program that will provide the greatest athletic transferability. Specific exercises that may lend themselves to complexes are Tire Flipping, Farmer's Walk, Sled Dragging, Super Yoke and a new category, loading events. In general, loading events in a traditional strongman setting come in the form of Stone Lifting. However, Stone Lifting events are not recommended for athletes in other sports, due to safety concerns and practical equipment issues. Instead, Sandbag and Keg Loading are the preferred options. Here are some effective combinations of these events:

Carry (Sandbag, FW, Super Yoke, Keg) and Drag (Sled)

Flip (Tire) and Drag (Sled)

Carry and Load (Sandbag, Keg)

These few movements can be combined into several different patterns depending upon the level of localized muscular endurance desired or how much lactic acid tolerance (i.e., "pain") the coach wishes to place upon the athlete.

Time Frames

A typical football lineman executes a play roughly once every 30 seconds. While the play itself is brief, the lineman must be conditioned to repeat this effort without a decrease in performance repeatedly throughout the course of an entire game – a condition often referred to as *accumulative fatigue*. Therefore, his alactic "capacity" must be on a par with his one-time alactic "power" to be effective during the game. To develop this quality, the following complex is recommended for a typical collegiate level lineman and for athletes in other sports that have subsequent increases in the time of execution.

Bottom Position Squat and Tire Flip Clusters

1 Bottom Position Squat or Blast Start

Immediately follow by 2 flips with a large (600+ pounds) tire

Total time for event completion: approximately 6-10 seconds

Rest 30 seconds between complexes and do 8-12 complexes

Rest 5 minutes between clusters and do 4-5 cluster sets

On any given play, the lineman may be required to block/shed a block multiple times, particularly if that play involves pursuit of any kind. The Bottom Position Squat will duplicate the neural demands to come off the start. The tire portion of this combination will simulate the subsequent blocks extremely well. However, grappling sports should use sandbags to simulate fighting an opponent.

Hockey

Because the work periods of wrestlers, football players, hockey players and soccer players vary significantly, work/rest ratios should be changed accordingly. Good strongman events include the Farmer's Walk (grip, unilateral movement, lower body/upper body-combined sport requirements) and Bent-Over Hamstring Drags (skating, local muscular endurance). Here is a sample workout:

Farmer's Walk, starting with an offset foot, for 150 feet (this will take approximately 25-35 seconds with a reasonable load)

Next, pick up the sled for the Bent Drags for a return trip of 150 feet

Total time to completion = approximately 45-50 seconds

Rest 90 to 120 seconds between sets

Repeat for 6 sets

The typical shift in ice hockey lasts 45 seconds, which is addressed by the 45-second load on the entire body with the combined Farmer's Walk and sled work. Stated more scientifically, the 45-second rest interval will mimic the lactic acid capacity demands of a standard shift rotation pattern seen in hockey games.

Baseball

While the true conditioning needs in baseball are minimal, speed and trunk power is required in short bursts of ball pursuit and hitting. Actual strength gains possible in the obliques have been shown to be limited, and in fact increases in hitting power come from lat strength gains. The unique nature of Single-Arm Drags addresses lat and shoulder stability. Ball- and bat-grip strength requirements are sufficiently addressed by the Farmer's Walk (grip, upper back, unilateral basis) and One-Arm Backwards Sled Drag (because it is a single-sided-dominant sport). Here is an effective routine for a baseball player:

Farmer's Walk for 150 feet (this could also be an Unbalanced Walk if muscular asymmetry is present)

One-Arm Backwards Sled Drags for return trip of 150 feet

Total time to completion = approximately 45 seconds

Soccer

The aerobic requirements for soccer are much higher than in most other sports, with much of the work coming in the form of short bursts of speed in many different directions. Each of these planes is addressed along with a longer time to completion for each set. The minimal work/rest ratio will generate a challenging interval training effect. Great exercises for soccer are the Side-to-Side Sled Drags (ab/adduction of hips) combined with Bent Hamstring Drags and then Backwards Sled Drags. Here is a good strongman workout for soccer:

Bent-Over Side-to-Side Sled Drags for 50 feet

Repeat facing in the opposite direction for another 50 feet

Bent Hamstring Drags for 150 feet

Backwards Drag for return trip of 150 feet

Total time to completion = approximately 60-90 seconds

Rest 4 minutes, then repeat

Complete 10 sets

Wrestling/Martial Arts (Tire Flip, Sandbag Load and Drag)

Workout I

By using a variety of muscle groups, blood lactate levels skyrocket. Every single muscle is involved in the following complex, and as such it is a great conditioner for athletes who do not have access to many different training partners for grappling work. As such, this workout will provide them with superior energy system work:

Tire Flip, 3 reps

Standing Log Press, 6 reps

Sled Face Pull, 6 steps each leg

Total time to completion = 40-60 seconds

Rest 3 minutes, then repeat

Complete 5 sets

In this workout and the one that follows, note that sled work is performed last. Sled work, especially Backwards Sled Drags, is always performed last due to the extreme fatigue and loss of stability it involves and to allow sufficient energy to perform other strongman events.

Workout II

This is a great complex to improve anaerobic lactic (alactic) capacity. Again, because of the multitude of muscles involved, lactate levels are unbearable. Every physical quality is developed, from explosive strength to the capacity to maintain speed in fatigued conditions. Here is the workout:

Standing Log Push Press, 4 reps

Super Yoke Side-to-Side pendulum motion, 6 steps each direction

Shotokan Backwards Walk, 6 steps per leg

Total time to completion = 60-70 seconds

Rest 3 minutes, then repeat

Perform 4 sets

In this section we provided several examples of complexes, but the number of effective complexes is limited only by a coach's imagination. As a rule of thumb, however, perform a specific complex for only six training sessions in a row before changing the complex.

POLIQUIN

Healthy. Lean. Strong.™

Chapter 7 • The Poliquin International Certification Program (PICP)

The Poliquin Strength Institute team is proud to present a new program to meet the needs of strength coaches throughout the world: The Poliquin International Certification Program (PICP).

The mission of the PICP is to improve the level of sports performance the world over through highquality strength coaching. We do this by providing coaches with the latest information on program design and teaching methodologies.

Program Levels

Levels 1 to 3 of the program are designed for strength coaches who work with developing athletes participating at levels ranging from regional to national. Each level of the PICP has three components: theory, technical and practical. The PICP issues a diploma upon completion of each component.

Levels 4 and 5 of the program are for well-established strength coaches interested in coaching at the international or professional sports level. Levels 4 and 5 are geared to highly qualified strength coaches. By the end of Level 5, the strength coach will have completed 12 requirements.

Level 1: Regional

THEORY (Theory Book)

Coaches learn how to identify all the different strength qualities. Then they learn the scientific basis of all the strength training loading parameters (e.g., reps, sets, tempo, rest interval, choice and order of exercise). Upon completing the manual, they are required to send in the provided written exam. The passing grade is 92 percent.

TECHNICAL (Program Design Seminar)

The technical component of Level 1 consists of a 16-hour course. The subject of the course is how to design effective strength programs, Level 1. At the end of the course, the written exam covers the evaluation of several specific training programs. The passing grade is 92 percent.

PRACTICAL (Internship at Poliquin Performance Center)

The practical component of Level 1 centers on evaluation of the strength qualities needed for effective training prescriptions. Coaches are integrated for two days into the training environment at the Poliquin Strength Institute and are assessed by qualified PICP staff (Master International Coach) at a regional center.

Level 2: State/Provincial

THEORY

Coaches learn the methodologies for training all the strength qualities: absolute strength, relative strength, explosive strength, reactive strength, starting strength and strength-endurance. For each methodology, coaches learn how to use the right tools, ranging from combined barbell/bungee cords to eccentric hooks. Upon completing the manual, they are required to send in the provided written exam. The passing grade is 92 percent.

TECHNICAL

The technical component of Level 2 consists of a 16-hour course. The subject of the course is how to design effective strength programs, Level 2. At the end of the course coaches are required to write three different programs for different cases. The passing grade is 92 percent.

PRACTICAL

The practical component of Level 2 centers on verifying the coaches' effectiveness at teaching strength training methodologies. Coaches are integrated for two days into the training environment at the Poliquin Strength Institute and are assessed by qualified PICP staff (Master International Coach) at a regional center.

Level 3: National

THEORY

Coaches learn new tools that assist in the training of national-caliber athletes. They are required to successfully complete the modules of the following six assignments:

- Training the energy systems
- Injury prevention and rehabilitation of lower extremities
- Injury prevention and rehabilitation of upper extremities
- Single-year periodization
- Applied functional strength
- Nutrition and supplementation

At the end of each assignment coaches take a written exam. The passing grade is 92 percent in every subject.

TECHNICAL

The technical component of Level 3 consists of a 16-hour course for which the goal is to complete a single-year periodization program wherein all physical qualities are addressed. The last part of the course includes an exam in which coaches design a training program for their own athletes.

PRACTICAL

The practical component of Level 3 provides coaches with feedback on their effectiveness when coaching in the weightroom. Each coach, along with his/her athlete, is integrated for five days into the training environment at the Poliquin Strength Institute and is assessed by qualified PICP staff (Master International Coach). Coaches are required to perform a series of assignments that week according to the athlete's needs. Only athletes from sports widely practiced on the international scene will be accepted.

At this level there is also a specific criterion for this component that must be met and be approved by the PICP: Coaches are required to prove that they have at least one athlete who followed their program, participated in a national championship and finished at 90 percent of the top three athletes.

To meet this criterion, a coach is required to submit to the PICP a letter from the National Sport Governing Organization confirming the participation and ranking of the athlete.

LEVEL 4: INTERNATIONAL

Level 4 represents one of the final steps of the PICP for coaches and is designed for those working with high-performance athletes and for those interested in pursuing a successful career in coaching. Level 4 consists of six assignments.

Coaches learn new tools that assist in the training of national-caliber athletes. They need to successfully complete the modules of the following six assignments:

- Biomechanics
- Time management
- External factors
- Quadrennial periodization
- Literature review on a strength topic
- Injury prevention and rehabilitation for the trunk

Only active coaches qualify for Level 4. Coaches need to complete the six assignments and also meet two of the following six criteria to obtain the PICP diploma for Level 4:

- Participate officially as a coach or an athlete at the Olympic Games
- Participate officially as a coach or an athlete at the World Championships
- Participate officially as a coach on the World Cup circuit
- Coach an athlete to the Senior World Championships
- Coach an athlete to the Olympic Games
- Coach an athlete on the World Cup circuit

Level 5: International Master Course Conductor

The highest goal in the Poliquin International Certification Program is to reach the International Master Course Conductor (IMCC) level. This level falls under jurisdiction of the Poliquin Strength Institute with the collaboration of the National Sport Governing Organization (NSGO). The identification of an IMCC needs the approval of both organizations. This level is competency-based according to the coach's experience and his form of education. The coaches who desire this level of certification have to submit their curriculum to the Poliquin Strength Institute. All curriculums are based on the achievement of the candidate. Only active coaches can qualify for this level. You need to meet four of the seven following criteria to obtain the IMCC qualification:

- Train a medalist at the Olympic Games
- Train a medalist at the Senior World Championships
- Participate officially as a coach or athlete at the Olympic Games or World Championships
- Train a World Record Holder in a recognized discipline
- Train an athlete who wins a distinguished award in the professional league: i.e., Norris (NHL), Cy Young (MLB)
- Develop course material for the PICP
- Work as a National Coach for 5 years

Note: *World Championships are for recognized disciplines where coaching is a factor: i.e., track and field, alpine skiing, volleyball, etc. Examples of sports not recognized are ice dancing, speed skiing.*